AIRE
BIKING GUIDE

Pocket Rides

①

Paul Hannon

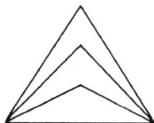

HILLSIDE

HILLSIDE
PUBLICATIONS
11 Nessfield Grove
Keighley
West Yorkshire
BD22 6NU

First published 1996

© Paul Hannon 1996

ISBN 1 870141 42 3

Illustrations
Front Cover: On Pinfold Hill, above Silsden
Back Cover: The Worth Valley
Page 1: Turkey Inn, Goose Eye
(Paul Hannon/Big Country Picture Library)

Printed in Great Britain by
Carnmor Print & Design
95-97 London Road
Preston
Lancashire
PR1 4BA

CONTENTS

SOME USEFUL ADDRESSES

Bradford Council Rights of Way Dept
Goulbourne Street, Keighley (01535-618317)

Tourist Information
2 West Lane **Haworth** (01535-642329)
Pictureville **Bradford** (01274-753678)
9 Sheep Street **Skipton** (01756-792809)

British Waterways (Leeds-Liverpool Canal)
Dobson Lock, Apperley Bridge, Bradford BD10 0PY
(01274-611303)

Cyclists' Touring Club
69 Meadrow, Godalming, Surrey GU7 3HS
(01483-417217)

British Cycling Federation
National Cycling Centre, Stuart Street, Manchester M11 4DQ
(0161-2302301)

British Rail, Leeds-Skipton line
Leeds (0113-244 8133)

Keighley & Worth Valley Railway
Haworth (01535-645214)

INTRODUCTION

On first impressions the Aire Valley is not abundantly laced with bridleways, but a good number have been found, researched and drawn into this guide. Each of these rides links bridleways and country lanes, with only a very minimum time spent on busier roads. The rides have been selected based not only on the restricted choice, but also on sensible, practical routes: the presence of a bridleway on the map doesn't guarantee it's worth using. Ground conditions vary with the season and the weather, though it is likely most people will be enjoying the majority of their outings in the warmer months. Don't be surprised to find a dry July run transformed into a muddy December struggle. None of these rides, however, should involve too much slutchy work, though in some cases there may be a very short spell where the only option, other than for a superhero, is to get off and push. Again, these have been kept to an absolute minimum: if we'd come to walk, we'd have our boots on!

The countryside of the Aire Valley is a splendid mix of farmland, moorland and woodland, and despite the dearth of bridleways these rides take in a remarkable variety of scenery. The views, too, are first-class, some extending to the higher country of the Yorkshire Dales. All of these routes feature uphill sections, though very little is particularly arduous. If you like flat country, move to Norfolk! Failing that, obtain your towpath permit and set about exploring the environs of the Leeds-Liverpool Canal, a splendid recreational asset. There is no general public right to cycle on towpaths, but limited sections are available, and one of these features in Route 5. A list of all permitted sections is supplied with your permit from British Waterways, along with a copy of the *Waterways Code for Cyclists*. They do request that groups of cyclists (other than small family groups) don't use the towpath, as these can cause obstructions to other users.

Using the guide
Each ride has its own little chapter, broken up into introductory details; route description; and features along the way (usually including one or two illustrations). A simple map gives a general picture of the route, the key being -

S start point   • • route   ⁄ roads   ◄ route direction

ᜪᜪᜪ canal   ᜪᜪᜪ railway   ↗ stream   ⠿ woodland

All rides are within the 8½-9 miles (13½-14½km) range, with the emphasis firmly on leisure riding rather than endurance test. Mention is sometimes made of shorter or easier options. The ratio of off-road to on-road riding is given for each run, but even the road work is almost exclusively on peaceful country lanes. Even taken at a steady pace, and savouring villages and sights en route, these runs fall into the category of a morning, afternoon or summer's evening ride: for families with younger members, I can confirm that the best part of a day might be allocated! Most pass a pub or two somewhere along the way, with other refreshment halts often available. Another useful feature is the indication of places of interest along the routes: not all guidebooks believe cyclists have any interest in their surroundings.

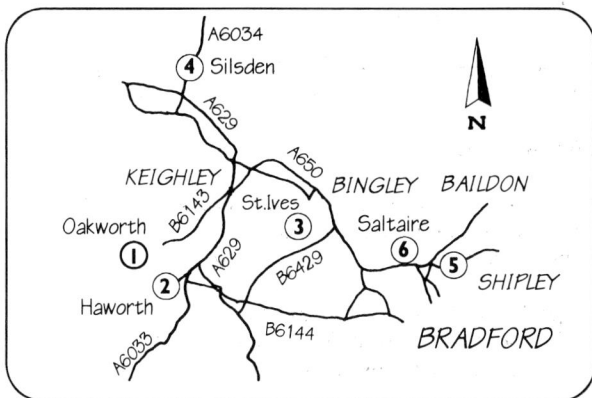

Sadly an irresponsible minority have given bikers a bad name in outdoor circles, which is rather unfortunate for the responsible majority. As a dedicated hillwalker, I too have had harsh words for mountain bikers carving up public footpaths in beautiful places. To be fair, many people are drawn to the countryside for the first time on acquiring a bike, and often are genuinely unaware of their rights and responsibilities. Hopefully the rides in the following pages will encourage more riders to enjoy a stimulating, entirely legal journey through our countryside, leaving no lasting sign of their passage. The Mountain Bike Code of Conduct is reproduced overleaf, and it incorporates the traditional Country Code. To sum up: ride with care, ride only where you are permitted, and ride with awareness of the environment and other users of the great outdoors.

THE MOUNTAIN BIKE CODE OF CONDUCT

RIGHTS OF WAY

- *Bridleways* - open to cyclists, but you must give way to walkers and horse riders.

- *Byways* - Usually unsurfaced tracks open to cyclists. As well as walkers and cyclists, you may meet occasional vehicles which also have a right of access.

- *Public footpaths* - no right to cycle exists.

Look out for posts from the highway or waymarking arrows (blue for bridleways, red for byways and yellow for footpaths).

OTHER ACCESS

- *Open land* - on most upland, moorland and farmland cyclists normally have no right of access without the express permission of the landowner

- *Towpaths* - a British Waterways cycling permit is required for cyclists wishing to use their canal towpaths
  (see introductory pages for details)

- *Pavements* - cycling is not permitted on pavements
  (though shepherding young children alongside a busy main road is unlikely to incur any problems)

- *Designated cycle paths* - look out for designated cycle paths or bicycle routes which may be found in urban areas, on Forestry Commission land, disused railway lines or other open spaces

OTHER INFORMATION

- Cyclists must adhere to the Highway Code. A detailed map is recommended for more adventurous trips.

THE COUNTRY CODE

- Enjoy the countryside and respect its life and work
- Guard against all risk of fire
- Fasten all gates
- Keep dogs under close control
- Keep to rights of way across farmland
- Use gates and stiles to cross fences, hedges and walls
- Leave livestock, crops and machinery alone
- Take your litter home
- Help to keep all water clean
- Protect wildlife, plants and trees
- Take special care of country roads
- Make no unnecessary noise

SAFETY

- Ensure that your bike is safe to ride and prepared for all emergencies
- You are required by law to display working lights after dark (front and rear)
- Always carry some form of identification
- Always tell someone where you are going
- Learn to apply the basic principles of first aid
- Reflective materials on your clothes or bike can save your life
- For safety on mountains refer to *Safety on Mountains,* a British Mountaineering Council publication
- Ride under control when going downhill, since this is often when serious accidents occur
- If you intend to ride fast off road it is advisable to wear a helmet
- Particular care should be taken on unstable or wet surfaces

START Oakworth   grid ref. SE 006381
The main road through Oakworth continues as the Colne road up through Pickles Hill to reach the Grouse Inn at Hare Hill. There is a parking/picnic area 200 yards past the pub.

DISTANCE 9 miles/14½km
Off road 3¾ miles/6km   **On road** 5¼ miles/8½km

TERRAIN Hilly country, but surprisingly only one (relatively short) appreciable rough climb. All the road work is on quiet country lanes, with glorious views over dark, drystone walls. An endearing feature of this district is the profusion of wooden seats placed at quiet corners: take full advantage of them!

ORDNANCE SURVEY MAPS
1:50,000 - Landranger 103, Blackburn & Burnley (tiny section)
104, Leeds, Bradford & Harrogate
1:25,000 - Outdoor Leisure 21, South Pennines

REFRESHMENTS
Pub at the start and at Goose Eye.

S Head back along the road to the *Grouse*, with its old windpump and glorious Bronteland views. Turn left on a walled track opposite. Beneath a wood, a modern tablet records the death of five Canadian airmen in 1944. Beyond, a junction is reached at Higher Turnshaw Farm. The rough lane (Turnshaw Road) continues straight ahead for Oakworth, but your way turns left here. This is White Lane, which soon becomes a surfaced road as it descends to a T-junction.

Ahead is the hamlet of **Newsholme**, and by turning right a few yards, a cul-de-sac road descends towards it. The route turns right after the first buildings at Green Bottom Farm. This narrow road loses its surface after the last farm and descends more roughly to join a road. Turn down into the hamlet of **Goose Eye** at the very foot of the hill.

Just past the *Turkey Inn* the road starts an uninviting pull: escape left on a track. Passing a branch to 'The Barn', the way swings sharply up to the left. Keep above the drive and the house on a slim bridleway that swings up to join the drive to Newsholme Dean. The valley of this name is outspread ahead, while the drive runs left, down towards the couple of houses. At the first building take a signposted fork right on a rougher track. Beyond the next gate it turns uphill for the rough section of the route, a climb with grand views over the deep valley. This stage sees it as an old sunken way. Above an old quarry the way becomes gentler with a flagged surface, joining another such track to rise to a road.

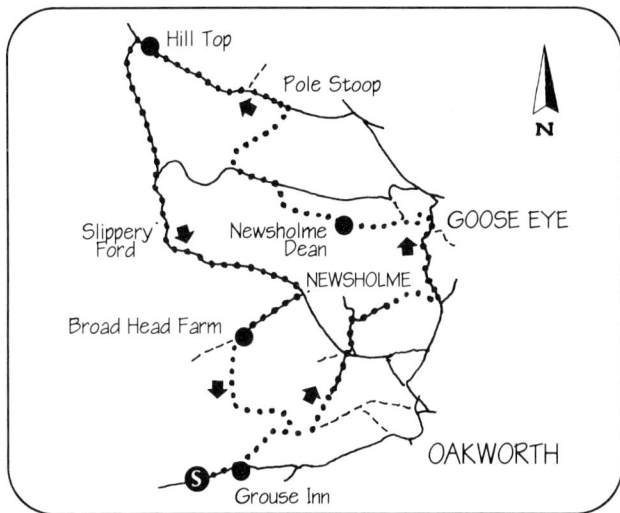

Turn left on Greystones Lane as far as a sharp bend. Here turn right on a short-lived enclosed way to a bridle-gate at the end. A gentle path crosses this large, rough pasture with a wall on the right to emerge onto the crest of **Pole Road** on the county boundary. Turn left to the next junction at Hill Top, with another inscribed stone and a West Riding guidepost: note the quaint spelling of Newsholme 'Dene'. Turn left, re-entering West Yorkshire for a steady run to the Slippery Ford farms. A narrow descent winds down to Morkin Bridge before a pull up and along White Hill. Views extend down the valley into Keighley backed by Rombalds Moor. At a crossroads, turn right up the cul-de-sac Broad Head Lane.

Past Broad Head Farm the lane becomes rougher: turn left along a short-lived drive. When it turns away continue on the wall-side track onto moor-like terrain. A good track traces the wall round to the left and onto a firmer footing approaching a wood corner. Keep on and bear right at the end to approach Tewitt Hall Farm. As the track turns left into the farm, take a gate to the right for a narrower descent between walls. This rejoins the outward route just five minutes short of the pub, and thus the start.

ALONG THE WAY

• *Newsholme* It is worth climbing into the cluster of buildings to appreciate the scene at Church Farm, semi-detached church and farm: a fascinating architectural and spiritual arrangement! Here also is another old windpump.

• *Goose Eye* is a former industrial hamlet sheltering in a deep hollow. It sprang to life again in the late 1970s with the opening of a tiny brewery in an old mill where paper for bank notes was once made. Now brewed in Keighley, these ales can normally be sampled at the ever popular Turkey Inn (illustrated on page 1).

• *Pole Road* The wall-side to Pole Road traces the North Yorkshire boundary, and at the same time earns extensive views northwards. Looking up the Aire Valley, Skipton is backed by Flasby Fell and Barden Moor, while beyond is a skyline of high Dales fells. Nearer to hand are the two monuments on Earl Crag above Cowling, while Keighley Moor stretches away to the left. Prominent on its skyline is the massive rock known as the Hitching Stone. On gaining Pole Road, note the mighty boundary stone of Pole Stoop over the wall opposite.

The Grouse Inn

START Haworth   grid ref. SD 030372
Start either from the church gates at the top of the main street
(car parks nearby).
Haworth is served by the Worth Valley Railway from Keighley.

DISTANCE 8½ miles/13½km
Off road 3½ miles/5½km   **On road** 5 miles/8km

TERRAIN A high level circuit of the valley enclosing Haworth
and Oxenhope. Steep early climbing is followed by a good mix
of moorland tracks and old lanes linked by quiet roads.

ORDNANCE SURVEY MAP
1:50,000 - Landranger 104, Leeds, Bradford & Harrogate
1:25,000 - Outdoor Leisure 21, South Pennines

REFRESHMENTS
Ample in Haworth. Pub at Leeming, pub/shops in Oxenhope.

S   From the church at the top of **Haworth**, descend the cobbled main street with care. At the bottom descend Bridgehouse Lane to the railway bridge. Turn right after it, up Brow Road. A steep pull leads to a crossroads with Hebden Road. Cross over and up Brow Top Road. Turn right at the first opportunity on Black Moor Road. This runs along the base of Brow Moor before becoming enclosed just after the solitary wind turbine by a quarry.

Remain on this road high above the valley until the rough Cuckoo Park Lane branches left (*Senior Way*). This emerges onto Black Moor, and a super run through the heather. There are good views over Cullingworth and the Aire Valley to a Rombalds Moor skyline. Above our impending route are the flapping sails of Ovenden Moor windfarm. This same track runs on through an old wall and along to a gate onto Trough Lane. Turn right to the *Dog & Gun*.

Cross the B6141 and up Sawood Lane. A steep pull leads past the dwellings at Sawood, becoming a rough track to join a Water Authority road. Enjoy sweeping views over Leeming and its reservoir to Oxenhope backed by Haworth's moors. Go right on this road, straight along the track as the road turns left to Thornton Moor Reservoir. Just beyond a *Bronte Way* guidepost the track turns left and forks.

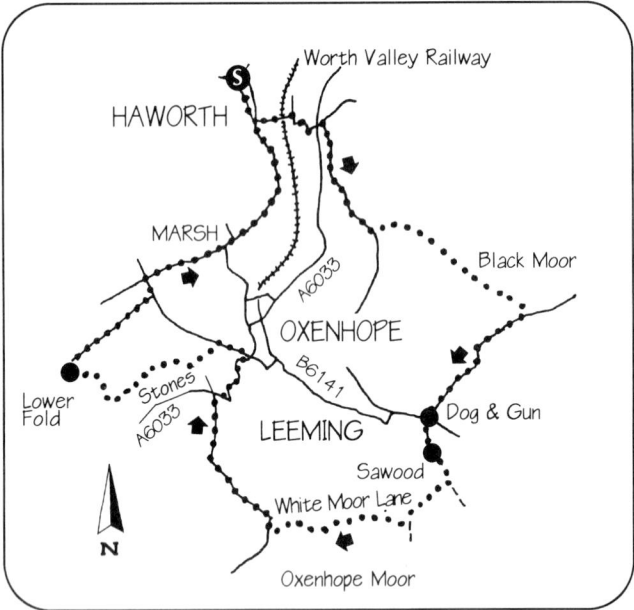

The left branch climbs between walls as Hambleton Lane, while yours, still Sawood Lane, runs with the wall going right, immediately starting a short descent. This quickly levels out and meanders along the moor, largely in good, but sometimes wet, terrain. Up to the left is a prominent cairn on the Nab, stood above old quarry workings and some distinctive sunken ways where stone would have been carted down by sledge.

The old road, now White Moor Lane, emerges onto surfaced Nab Water Lane. Turn right, soon enjoying a long, steep descent. The latter stage is particularly steep, so caution is needed. Brake in good time at the bottom as you are joining the A6033 Hebden Bridge road. Note an inscribed guidepost on the left at the junction. *The inviting way straight across the main road cannot be recommended as currently it has no official status. The rough lane leads to the pocket moorland of Stones, an urban common, where level with the lone house a clear path bears left across the centre of the moor: this quickly starts to slant down towards Stones Farm to join our route on the old 'road' there.*

The Dog & Gun

Turn right down the A6068 through a hairpin bend and into the top end of **Oxenhope**. Descend past the church to a junction with Shaw Lane (the *Bay Horse* is 100 yards further on the main road). Go left on Shaw Lane. A direct route keeps straight on to climb to a junction with Marsh Lane. The longer, off-road route turns left up narrow Stone Lane at a kink in Shaw Lane near the end of the houses. After a steep little pull this becomes a broad track along the foot of the pocket moorland known as Stones. At the far corner this old 'road' becomes enclosed by walls and this next stage calls for awareness of other users, for though the walls remain set well apart, the way is at times only a thin path between undergrowth.

The track winds down to the bottom of Rag Clough then climbs above a water conduit. This rocky section is likely to induce a short spell of pushing. A short pull, partly flagged, sees the way improve and swing left to approach Lower Fold. It joins a drive between the buildings, turning right on it then sharp right almost at once to head away. This lane becomes surfaced for a long, steady descent as Outside Lane to rejoin Shaw Lane alongside the old Hawksbridge Methodist Chapel. Go left to the crossroads just above, then right along Marsh Lane. This provides an easy finish, passing through the scattered settlement of Marsh before dropping down to conclude the run along Sun Street, meeting the foot of the cobbled main street just past the *Old Hall*, now a hotel. The station is down to the right, and the church up to the left.

Main Street, Haworth

ALONG THE WAY

• **Oxenhope** is a fine example of what was once a thriving Pennine mill community. The Worth Valley Railway ends here, confirming its original purpose in serving the mills, but the village lets its illustrious neighbour Haworth deal with the tourist hordes. The station features a railway museum. A popular and now famous local event is the annual straw race in July, a colourful pub crawl which is a great charity fund-raiser.

• **Haworth** ceased to be just another village in the 19th century when the fame of the Brontes spread, though it took until relatively recently to become a full-blown tourist honeypot. Focal point is the cobbled main street, lined with gift shops and tearooms and climbing steeply to the parish church. Surrounded by pubs, only its tower remains from the Brontes' day, but hidden behind it is the parsonage, now a museum in honour of its former occupants. Most famous of a talented family were the three sisters Charlotte, Emily and Anne, and best known of their output were the novels Jane Eyre and Wuthering Heights. At the bottom of town is the other major attraction, the Keighley and Worth Valley Railway. Altough this preserved steam line runs from Keighley to Oxenhope, Haworth station, with its goods yard, is the hub of things.

Bronte Parsonage

START St. Ives   grid ref. SE 094389
Start from the estate car park, off either the Bingley-Harden road or the Keighley-Harden road. Railway station in Bingley, 1 mile.

DISTANCE 8½ miles/13½km
Off road 5 miles/8km   **On road** 3½ miles/5½km

TERRAIN A switchback route through the villages around Harden Beck. Very varied terrain, but almost entirely rideable.

ORDNANCE SURVEY MAPS
1:50,000 - Landranger 104, Leeds, Bradford & Harrogate
1:25,000 - Pathfinder 682, Bradford

REFRESHMENTS
Pubs/shops in Harden, Wilsden, Cullingworth: also the Guide Inn.

S From **St. Ives** car park by the play area take the road rising to the golf club. It swings left between the mansion and the course. Keep straight on this estate road, passing the new clubhouse and the attractive stable block at Home Farm, and remain on the road (speed ramps) through trees and out to the Keighley road by St. Ives Lodge. Turn steeply downhill into **Harden**, then left down the main street and right along Wilsden Road. This descends to cross Harden Beck at the *Malt Shovel*, an inn with a great deal of history and a remarkable floral display.

The road climbs steeply towards Wilsden as Harden Lane, but is left at the first chance by a rough lane on the left. Sandy Banks lives up to its name as it winds steeply up through woods. Above a quarry at Bank Top, Lee Lane begins, and a level run, half road, half track, leads to a junction. Turn right on Cross Lane, and when the road turns left keep straight on the bridleway (still Cross Lane) leading unerringly to **Wilsden**. The steep, rocky middle section contrasts with the otherwise broad, level track.

The main street is joined along Smithy Lane. Turn left up it and first right along Chapel Row. This starts to climb as Wilsden Hill Road, and is left at the first chance by Tan House Lane along to the right. This leaves the houses behind and rises past a tiny cluster of houses at Pye Bank, then suddenly climbs a bank as a narrow pathway. A quick return to firm, level track is made at the top, and a splendid contour around the hillside. Ahead are the impressive arches of the abandoned Hewenden Viaduct.

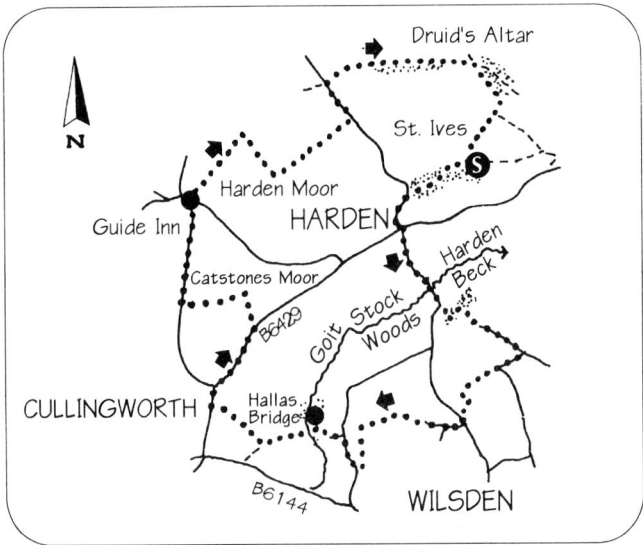

At the end a narrow lane is joined. Double back right down this as far as a rough cul-de-sac lane steeply down to the left. This leads to Hallas Bridge cottages. Bear left down a steep, narrow path to Hallas Bridge in **Goit Stock Woods**. With no walkers around it may be possible to gain sufficient momentum for the steep climb up the narrow path of Hallas Lane opposite, which quickly relents as a hard surfaced way. As several popular paths branch off, be aware of pedestrians.

The going eases and the way broadens into a rough lane by Hallas Hall Farm. Head along this until suburban Greenside Lane turns off right. This runs on to join the main street in **Cullingworth**. Turn right, the road descending to the Keighley Road turning which offers an easier alternative to the next off-road section: just follow it all the way up to the *Guide Inn*. Otherwise, remain on the main road through Cow House Bridge and on as far as the narrow bridleway of Dolphin Lane on the left. This gives an enclosed climb between brambles and undergrowth. Though it can be largely ridden, the main problem is passing any fellow users.

Escape at the top onto the foot of heathery Catstones Moor. Turn left along its base, a good track leading to a gate off the moor, where it becomes enclosed to emerge onto Keighley Road. Turn right, the steady gradient soon easing to reach the *Guide Inn*. Care is needed on the blind brow of this junction, a curious crossroads. The *Guide* has long been a popular hilltop hostelry: note the great picture on the outside wall.

Departure is by none of the roads, but a rough lane just above the pub. This leads onto Harden Moor, and continues as a broad track along the moor edge. Views ahead feature a Rombalds Moor skyline, Baildon Hill and Shipley. The only instruction is to remain with the left-hand wall: at the first corner a bridleway bears left off the moor, but a permissive bridleway offers a far nicer route. This turns right, remaining between wall and moor for a super ride.

At the next corner it drops to encounter a rough, narrow section above Deep Cliff Hole. Extreme caution is needed here, more for the presence of walkers than your own safety! In fact it is a good testing section, the object being to avoid all the slabby gritstone rocks. An easy path re-asserts itself to follow the wall along to the Keighley-Harden road. Opposite is the mighty wall enclosing St. Ives estate. Turn left for a couple of minutes to the brow, then take the rough Altar Lane to the right. Ahead are fine views to Rombalds Moor high above Riddlesden and East Morton. The old road is rough but firm as it descends steadily outside the estate wall. When it meets a junction a gate admits to the estate. First though, it is worth dumping your bike in the undergrowth for a five minute stroll along the waymarked path to the **Druids' Altar**.

Back at the junction, turn through the gate and follow the broad track down to the left. At weekends this is a very popular spot for family walks, so take care: please also remember that not all the tracks within the estate are bridleways. At a barn the main track swings right, and as Cross Gates Lane leads down to the estate road between the clubhouse and Home Farm. Turn left for the car park.

18

ALONG THE WAY

• **St. Ives** was owned by the Knights Templars and Knights Hospitallers, and later by the monks of Rievaulx Abbey. The estate passed to the Ferrands in 1636, and into public ownership in 1928. The 19th century mansion has been renovated as a nursing home. Sharing these hundreds of acres with the public are a farm, golf course and turf research centre.

• **Harden** is a sizeable village strongly linked with Bingley. It is dominated by large factories and modern housing. The Golden Fleece pub stands just up the main street.

• **Wilsden** is a street village of gritstone cottages fast becoming a large commuter settlement. It climbs for a good mile to Lingbob on the Haworth-Bradford road, and boasts several inns all too far up the street for us.

• **Goit Stock Woods** are a local beauty spot, especially resplendant in springtime. Hallas Bridge is a modest structure on Harden Beck: it is just a five minute walk downstream to view the delightful Goit Stock Falls.

• **Cullingworth** is the third and final village, yet another mix of old mills, cottages and modern housing. An immediate left fork by the Wesleyan Methodist Chapel of 1824 (note the impressive sundial) reveals a cobbled corner featuring the tall spired church and the George Inn.

• **The Druids' Altar** is modest gritstone edge which reveals the busy floor of the Aire Valley as a foreground to the slopes and moors behind. If the Druids did offer sacrifices here, they certainly chose a grand spot.

The Guide Inn

START Silsden   grid ref. SD 041464
Start in the town centre. Car park and roadside parking.
Steeton & Silsden station is 1 mile distant.

DISTANCE 9 miles/14½km
Off road 4 miles/6½km   **On road** 5 miles/8km

TERRAIN Largely easy, with four distinct sections.
A straightforward opening section to Riddlesden; a long
road climb to the moor edge; an undulating country
run along the top; and a rapid return by narrow lanes.

ORDNANCE SURVEY MAPS
1:50,000 - Landranger 104, Leeds, Bradford & Harrogate
1:25,000 - Outdoor Leisure 21, South Pennines (from 1995
edition, otherwise Pathfinder 671, Keighley & Ilkley)

REFRESHMENTS
Ample in Silsden. Nothing en route
unless detouring into Riddlesden.

S Head south along the main street and just before the bridge over the Leeds-Liverpool Canal, turn left at Clog Bridge (for Howden Road). Take the first right (Hainsworth Road) which passes under the canal. Keep left at a junction by new housing and remain on this road, immediately into the country along a hedgerowed lane. Keep on to its demise at Howden House, where a firm drive takes the bridleway on to Low Holden Farm.

Pass straight through on the left side of the buildings, and a green track heads away. This quickly becomes encased in foliage, rising left to run beneath the canal embankment. At a vague fork the way goes right (Keighley golf course is just over the wall), on an unconvincingly thinner path through the undergrowth of no-man's-land. This quickly restores itself to a good track beneath the towpath again, swinging right to a junction on the edge of the golf course. While a footpath turns right to cross the course, your track rises left to the canal bank.

Cross the bridge and turn up the broad track right to Riddlesden golf glub. With the clubhouse to the left, turn right along the drive, which splits within yards, at a car park. Take the right branch which drops away and runs undulatingly along as Elam Wood Road above the wooded canal bank. Beware speed ramps as you ride on to emerge very suddenly into suburban **Riddlesden**. This is Scott Lane West, and at the end a multiple junction offers a choice.

Heroes can opt for the stiff pull up Slade Lane (locally Kiln Bank) which climbs to Banks Lane. Most will take the slightly less steep Dunkirk Rise, doubling back sharp left. At the top turn right up Western Avenue. This too climbs to Banks Lane, so however you got here, turn left and climb out into the country, the gradients slowly easing to reach a T-junction under **Rivock Edge**. A wooden bench offers welcome relief: the climb is over!

Turn left along the road (Holden Lane), noting the opportunity of a direct return to Silsden. Your route leaves it, however, at the second bridleway on the right. It comes just after passing the house of Holden Gate, hidden in foliage. The bridleway starts at a gate at a lay-by, and heads away as a green, wall-side track rising to a wall-corner on **Pinfold Hill**.

The inviting track leaves the wall-corner and slants down to a gate at the bottom corner, then descends above a wall to pass along the top side of the farm at Rough Holden. Beyond its enclosures remain on the wall-side track, but navigate with caution here to take a branch left on approaching a fence. This is the key to a gate in the bottom corner. Descend a faint wall-side track, bearing right half-way down to join a wall slanting right into **Holden Gill**. A clearer track forms towards the corner. Pass above a pond, through gorse to a gate at the end. The track drops down to cross Holden Beck by a ford. Upstream are a footbridge and a water pipeline.

The track goes left to the wall, then fades as a steep climb traces it to the top corner. From the gate there an enclosed track rises the few yards to Ghyll Grange. Pass left of the buildings as the track swings round to join the farm drive. Another easier finish (you'll be back in ten minutes) is to go left along it and follow the lane down through Brunthwaite.

• *Riddlesden* boasts two fine houses. Over to the right at the junction is the private West Riddlesden Hall, lesser known cousin to East Riddlesden Hall, a mile distant on the main road. The latter is a magnificent gritstone manor house dating from 1640, sitting on a wooded knoll overlooking the river Aire. It is a National Trust property and well worth a visit.

East Riddlesden Hall

The main route turns right. Follow waymarks through the yard and past the house (this is preferred to the definitive route, which passes through an enclosure left of the buildings). As the concrete drive forks, pass a branch to the big house ahead and keep left a little further to a walled track rising left. Ending in a field, trace the left-hand wall to meet a drive as it joins a sharp bend of a road. Go straight on Light Bank Lane beneath White Crag. At the end go left on Brownbank Lane which soon starts to descend. Part way down, go left on Swartha Lane. This winds through the hamlet of Swartha to descend to a T-junction on the suburban edge of Silsden. Go right on Howden Road to finish.

ALONG THE WAY

• **Rivock Edge** is a prominent moorland brow, a major Keighley landmark now partly obscured by forestry. Bronze age Cup and ring marked rocks are scattered about its escarpment. Extensive views look over Keighley and up the Worth Valley to the Haworth moors.

• **Pinfold Hill** is a minor brow and a superb place to linger. A few modest outcrops of gritstone offer a perfect backrest or foreground to savour a stunning prospect of South Craven and the Aire Valley. Lunds Tower on Earl Crag above Cowling leads the eye to Pendle Hill, while up the valley are higher Dales fells. Sandwich time!

• **Holden Gill** is, notably downstream of your crossing, a charming wooded dell. The Victorians who came to savour its 'quaint' charms would find refreshments being offered at Ghyll Grange, which centuries earlier was a grange of nearby Bolton Priory. The pipeline was constructed by Bradford Corporation to convey water from their Nidderdale reservoirs to the thirsty city.

In Holden Gill

START Shipley   grid ref. SE 154379
From the central crossroads (Fox Corner) turn down the A6038
Otley road, through a roundabout and right at traffic lights onto
Dockfield Road. Start from the canal swing bridge. Further
parking along Dockfield Road. Railway station in Shipley.

DISTANCE 9 miles/14½km
Off road 6½ miles/10½km   **On road** 2½ miles/4km

TERRAIN An undemanding, near level ride. Main features of the
route are the canal towpath on the outward leg, and the village
of Esholt on the return, reached largely by good tracks and quiet
roads. Particularly suitable as a family ride, for even the two
very brief main road sections have adjacent footways.

ORDNANCE SURVEY MAPS
1:50,000 - Landranger 104, Leeds, Bradford & Harrogate
1:25,000 - Pathfinder 671, Keighley & Ilkley; 682, Bradford

REFRESHMENTS
Ample in Shipley; pubs at Apperley Bridge and Esholt.

• *IMPORTANT* - ensure you have a valid towpath permit displayed
before you set out (see introductory pages).

🅢 As the first tiny section of towpath from the canal swing bridge is
'out of bounds', continue along Dockfield Road just as far as a railway
bridge. At Bridge 210 alongside, join the now broader towpath of the
Leeds-Liverpool Canal. A splendid ride follows, so near urban sur-
rounds yet seemingly well out in the country, particularly as Thackley
Woods come to cloak the opposite bank after the railway has
departed. The first bridge passed is worth noting: it is at this point you
will rejoin the towpath to finish, on the path coming up from the left.

For now remain on the towpath, which runs in a great curve in tandem
with the Aire over to the left. Another railway bridge signals its
emergence from Thackley Tunnel. When the British Waterways office

at Dobson Lock is reached, the access road runs out to a road bridge at Apperley Bridge. Here vacate the canal and turn down to the left. At the junction at the *George & Dragon* turn left over the old bridge to join the A658 Bradford-Harrogate road alongside the *Stansfield Arms*.

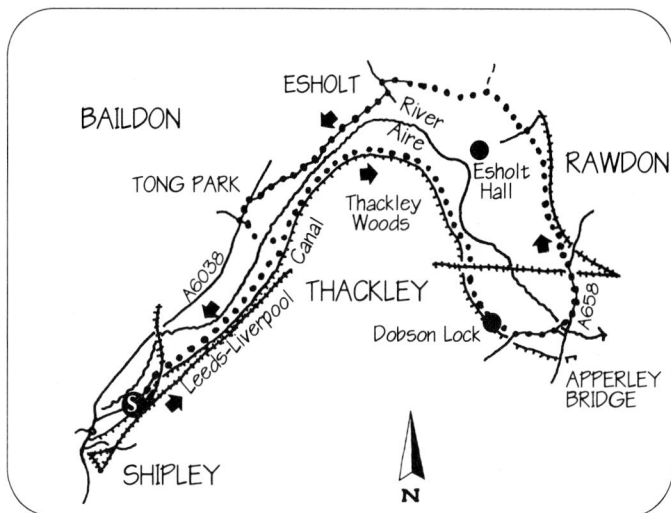

Head up this road towards Rawdon, passing the *Queens* on the right and the drive to Esholt Hall on the left. Yards further, opposite Apperley Manor Hotel, take what appears to be a short private drive on the left. Turn right off it almost at once on a path into woodland. This same path runs pleasantly through trees beneath the railway line, with Esholt treatment works largely masked (visually at least) by the trees. On joining a road, go left just a few yards and resume on a broader track opposite to arrive at a junction. Bear left and straight on again, still with woodland on the right to soon join a waterworks road. With the works now in their full glory continue along this road to enter **Esholt** village. The main street is just down to the left.

Leave by the lower road out, starting as Chapel Lane and becoming Esholt Lane. This runs on in the company of the river Aire before winding away to join the A6038 opposite the *Shoulder of Mutton* at Tong Park. Go left for less than a minute to a junction with Roundwood Road, and here escape left along the slender Buck Lane. As it descends to some houses, bear right down a broad path which runs enclosed down to a footbridge on the Aire. An iron notice on it announces that it was provided by the Idle and Baildon authorities in 1889 for the footpath and bridleway linking the two communities. The path up the other side (Buck Mill Lane) rejoins the canal towpath to retrace the opening mile and a half back to Bridge 210 and onto Dockfield Road.

ALONG THE WAY
• **Esholt** is a tiny village, until the advent of TV soaps known only for its vast sewage works. Indeed, some critics have drawn cruel parallels with Esholt's two dubious outputs! The village centre is very attractive in its own right however, with its pub the Commercial now permanently known as the Woolpack, and the lovely Old Hall tucked down a side street. Just past it is the hidden church. Esholt Hall, in the hands of the water authority, stands on the site of a Cistercian priory.

• **The Leeds-Liverpool Canal** was completed in 1816, though this easternmost section was operating by 1777. It runs for 127¼ miles and remains entirely navigable. Its builders exploited the Aire Gap to take this northernmost and longest of the trans-Pennine canals across the country's backbone. A vast number of locks was necessary to lift the waterway through the hills without need for major tunnels. Though built to serve the commerce of the many towns along its route, its working life was cut short by the arrival of the far more efficient railways. Today it is a growing leisure amenity with anglers, walkers and boaters its chief users. Walk a few yards towards Shipley to see the old bridge here illustrated.

Canal bridge,
Shipley

START Saltaire   grid ref. SE 139379
Off road parking and railway station.

DISTANCE 8½ miles/13½km
Off road 5¼ miles/8½km   **On road** 3¼ miles/5km

TERRAIN Mostly easy, with one short, rough push early on.
The remainder is largely good tracks and moorland roads.
The early rough climb above Loadpit Beck can be avoided by
starting at Shipley Glen and taking the glen road to reach the
Golcar track: this also reduces the trip to under 7 miles.

ORDNANCE SURVEY MAPS
1:50,000 - Landranger 104, Leeds, Bradford & Harrogate
1:25,000 - Pathfinder 671, Keighley & Ilkley; 682, Bradford

REFRESHMENTS
Pub and cafe at Saltaire; pubs at Eldwick and at High Eldwick
(just off-route); pub and tearoom at Shipley Glen.

S   Leave **Saltaire** by descending Victoria Road past the railway
station and Congregational Church. At the bottom cross the bridge
over the Leeds-Liverpool Canal to the *Boat House Inn*. A large
pedestrian bridge (***no cycling, so please get off and push!***) crosses the
Aire to Roberts Park. A little more walking is necessary to join Higher
Coach Road at the first opportunity, with the *Cup & Ring* pub along
to the right. Bear left on Higher Coach Road past the park and school
and on by housing. After passing the store, just before the road
becomes a track, take a narrow, enclosed path to the right. This rises
to a fork: go left into the woods, generally level to reach another fork
with a wall corner and open field on the left. Take the left branch,
dropping down to reach the foot of a small dam on Loadpit Beck.

The narrow rocky section up the other side demands a short push to
attain easier ground. As the gradient eases a part cobbled course takes
over, and the way rises out of the wood and to the start of a rough drive.

Baildon Moor is over to the right. Follow this lane past Sheriff Farm, then branch right along Lode Pit Lane. Follow this to a junction with a surfaced lane, and bear left, keeping straight on above the beck to emerge as Saltaire Road on the edge of Eldwick village.

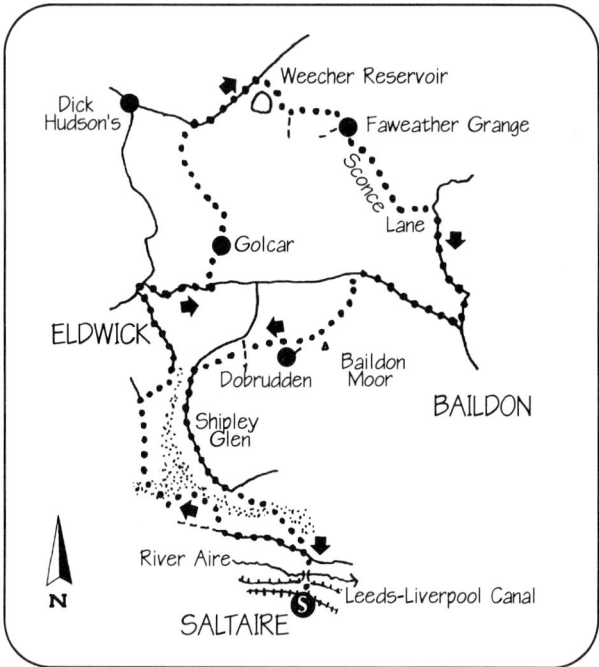

Turn right down to the beck. Along the Green is the *Acorn Inn*, while your route takes first right, Spring Lane. Follow this up around a dodgy corner and onto the level. At the Baildon boundary sign where Glovershaw Lane takes over, take a drive on the left rising straight to Golcar Farm. Pass along the front of the house to a gate, then an enclosed track rises up to the left. This gentle climb emerges into a field at a bridle-gate. Go left with the wall to the next gate, then continue alongside a fence to a wall corner in front. Go right with the wall, up through a gate and one more field to join Whitecroft farm drive. This rises to join Otley Road. Two minutes along to the left is the renowned pub, ***Dick Hudson's***.

Go right for half a mile, up round the corner and on as far as the turning right for Weecher Reservoir. The access road winds down to a corner beyond the reservoir: take the rougher track forking left. Keep on this to descend to a couple of houses. Take the track branching left through a gate to the farm at **Faweather Grange**. The track - Sconce Lane - runs on in grand style, past a scout camp to emerge onto a road. Go right onto the foot of Baildon Moor, and up past the *Whitehouse* pub/restaurant to an Ordnance Survey column and car park. The road runs down towards Baildon village, but take the first right on Bingley Road to stay on the moor. After a short climb to the brow, turn left along the rough road to Dobrudden. On this brow the Ordnance Survey column on Baildon Hill, summit of **Baildon Moor**, is seen to the left, while on the right are the cinder caves.

Immediately after the caves leave the road as it descends to Dobrudden caravan site, and take an inviting path bearing right for the wall corner ahead. Descend to the next corner, with the upper reaches of **Shipley Glen** revealed below. This is the only steeper rough downhill section, as the track delves into the bracken. A cautious descent will ensure the track is not further eroded. It crosses the Crook Farm road then resumes more gently to run along to the glen road at another wall corner.

The Boathouse, Saltaire

Go left here, cruising along to the *Old Glen House* pub. En route you pass the Soldiers' Trench stone circle and Bracken Hall Countryside Centre. Alongside the pub is a tearoom. Keep straight on Prod Lane, descending past a funfair to the top station of the Shipley Glen tramway. Turn down its near-side on a parallel, surfaced path (beware young families) to emerge back onto Higher Coach Road. Go left to finish.

ALONG THE WAY

•**Saltaire** is the mill village of Sir Titus Salt, who in 1850 began hundreds of terraced stone dwellings to house the workforce of his new worsted processing mill. This outstanding piece of industrial architecture, 550ft long and 6 storeys high, is a sight to behold. The village's grid-iron system remains intact, along with the schools, almshouses, hospital and institute that followed. Almost all the buildings function much as Salt originally intended, and together form a major conservation area. Finest of Salt's buildings is the remarkable Congregational Church, built in 1859 in rich Italian style with a semicircular front and ornate circular tower.

Saltaire
Congregational
Church
(United Reformed
Church)

• **Dick Hudson's** (the Fleece) is named after the proprietor, who ran it for 30 years from 1850. In Victorian and Edwardian times workers from the smoky cities made this a place of pilgrimage. Easter weekend was the busiest of times, when they came in their hordes via Bingley and Saltaire to stride out for the moors, often crossing to Ilkley and back in the day: their inevitable breaks for refreshment were here, usually on both legs of the journey. The inn served travellers from early morning to late at night, most popular fare being a Yorkshire speciality, ham and egg teas. Only in relatively recent times has the practise really diminished. The present building dates from around 1900, though the original inn would have served the packhorse trade long before the millworkers ever came.

• **Baildon Moor** is the site of Bronze age earthworks, and was mined for coal from at least 1387: the 'cinder caves' on the summit of the moor are resulting slagheaps. The moor was purchased by Bradford Corporation for £7000 in 1897, and sees every activity: the ungainly posturing of hang-gliders is particularly entertaining. In the 1920s it was even the scene of illegal gambling rings. The moor is a fine viewpoint for the Aire Valley and the Pennine watershed.

• **Shipley Glen** has been a place of popular resort since people first escaped city grime for weekend fresh air. Its proximity to the Bradford metropolis has always ensured a regular stream of visitors. The Soldiers' Trench is a Bronze age double circle of at least 60 stones. Bracken Hall Countryside Centre has local history and wildlife displays. The Shipley Glen Cable Tramway was built in 1895 to haul visitors up the wooded bank to the attractions of the glen.

• **Faweather Grange** was originally a small grange of Rievaulx Abbey. It has been an important meeting place for centuries since, with packhorse routes coming from all directions. The monks

mined iron-stone nearby, while a new stone mine was opened as recently as 1889 and worked to a depth of 90 feet for flags and roofing stone.

LOG OF THE RIDES

No	Date	Start	Finish	Notes
1				
2				
3				
4				
5				
6				